Victorian and Edwardian

WARWICKSHIRE

from old photographs

1
King Edward VII planting an oak tree
in Rugby School Close, watched by the
headmaster, Dr H. A. James, July 1909

Victorian and Edwardian

WARWICKSHIRE

from old photographs

Introduction and commentaries by
DOROTHY H. McCULLA
and
MARTIN HAMPSON

B. T. BATSFORD LTD
LONDON

First published 1976
Reprinted 1983
Text copyright D. McCulla and M. Hampson 1976

Designed by Eddie Gleeson

Filmset by Servis Filmsetting Ltd, Manchester
Printed by The Anchor Press, Tiptree, Essex
for the publishers, B. T. Batsford Limited
4 Fitzhardinge Street
London W1H 0AH

ISBN 0 7134 3101 6

2
The Royal house party at Packington,
the house of Lord Aylesford, in November 1874. Both Prince Edward (later
Edward VII) and Princess Alexandra
were present

CONTENTS

3
Members of the Birmingham Photographic Society waiting to go into action. To 'shoot' Warwickshire, these intrepid gentlemen would travel by cable tram and railway with tripod and heavy plate camera. Dr Alan Whitehouse, the son of George Whitehouse, one of the original contributors to the Warwickshire Photographic Survey, kindly produced some useful notes: The exterior views required fairly long exposures running into several seconds. The interior views necessitated stopping down the lens still more and in a room that was dark the exposure could be about ten minutes. With six double dark slides there would be a dozen plates to develop on their return home. . . . their dark room was at the top of the house without a water supply, so it was a case of carrying up a large enamelled can of water from the bathroom on the floor below

ACKNOWLEDGMENTS

We wish to thank the following for their kind permission to use photographs from their collections: Birmingham Reference Library (3–5, 7, 8, 10–12, 14–16, 18, 22–27, 33–34, 36, 38, 40–41, 44, 46–48, 50, 52–54, 57–58, 61–66, 68–69, 71–72, 75–84, 87–95, 97–99, 103, 105, 107, 109, 111–113, 115–120, 122–123, 125, 128–129, 136–138, 140, 142–143, 147–153); Leamington Spa Museum & Art Gallery (6); Leamington Spa Public Library (21, 42, 146); Nuneaton Public Library (45, 145); Rugby Public Library (1, 49, 86, 114, 130–131, 134–135, 139); Solihull Public Library (39, 102, 126); Stratford-upon-Avon Record Office, Mr R. Bearman (43, 59, 60, 70, 74); Warwick Record Office, Michael Farr, archivist and Colin Hughes (9, 30, 73, 106, 141); Earl of Aylesford (2); Ursula Bloom (67, 144) Colin Green (19, 32, 37, 51, 55, 56, 96, 108); Henley-in-Arden Guildhall, Mr F. S. Lodder (104, 110, 132); David Jewsbury & Charles Lines (13, 20, 121, 133); Mansell Collection (17); Dr S. Tibbits (127); Warwickshire Div. Police (100, 101). We also wish to thank Miss J. Morris (Warwick Museum) for advice and Mr W. G. Belsher for rephotographing much of the material appearing here.

4
The affairs of Astley, near Nuneaton, discussed by a stile worn smooth by the palms. The large gentleman was probably George Lucas, parish clerk and postmaster. Not far from this peaceful scene men are working in the coal-pits. The church of Astley once possessed a fine tall steeple, which helped to guide travellers through the dense woodlands. It was known as 'the lantern of Arden'. 1896

INTRODUCTION

This shire is sited neare unto the heart of all England and therefore participates with her in the best both for aire and soile wanting nothing for profit or pleasure for man.

Many changes have taken place since these words were written by John Speed nearly four centuries ago, but happily even the ravages of time cannot remove Warwickshire from its natural place in the heart of the kingdom. The whole region, which measures some 50 miles from North to South and about 33 miles in breadth, is divided into two distinct areas, the Arden woodland to the North and the open field or Feldon to the South. As the Victorian age advanced the southern region of the County remained mainly rural, but within the northern region two distinct industrial sections developed. The coal mining industry and the brick and clay manufactures flourished in the eastern part, while on the western side, the town of Birmingham inexorably developed from a market town into an industrial metropolis.

For centuries the Arden woodland provided a refuge for hunted men and beasts and within Warwickshire folk lies the instinct to protect and preserve the ancient trees and their descendants which happily still shelter the County in places, to form the winding leafy lanes which bind hamlet and village together and so provide the County with its most distinctive feature. Sturdy trees of oak and elm stand tall in hawthorn hedges. Their branches are used to make the characteristic five-barred gates which divide the tangled mass of blackthorn, honeysuckle and dog-roses. Although Warwickshire is an inland county, each Autumn sea-birds from the Bristol Channel penetrate the thickets of willow, sedges and rushes which encrust the banks of the County's principal river, the deep muddy Avon. It is a part of England which enjoys great variety: from ancient castles and moated houses, humble villages with their pretty cottages, quiet churches and quaint mills, to the desolation of pit rubbish and winding gear of mining areas, the bustle and din of industrial towns, and to the honest respectability of the red-brick Victorian villas which spread fingerlike into the rural areas. Warwickshire is rich in historical and literary associations as well as being renowned for agricultural reform and industrial invention.

The main roads of Warwickshire, which were well constructed of limestone and gravel from local quarries, greatly assisted the coachmen of the early Victorian age. These men had to sit on a draughty box for ten hours a day; they even stuffed their shirt-fronts with paper in the winter-time to keep out the cold. They were often the harbingers of news and carriers of parcels between mothers and their children at work in the town, and they collected such town commodities as tea and sugar from young people in service, who endeavoured to send good things back to their relatives in the country. As the century advanced the good roads rendered the new sport of bicycling easy and enjoyable through the undulating gentle scenery. Indeed in the City of Coventry cycle-making superseded the manufacture of sewing machines in the 1860s. Towards the end of the nineteenth century the first motor car was produced in Coventry by Daimler. Once more Warwickshire people had to face a new invention in their twisting lanes.

Varied architecture and types of building materials can still be seen within the County. Old farmhouses and cottages were built of timber, plaster and bricks made from local clay and marl. The old clay thatched cottage generally had three compartments; a general living room/kitchen and two bedrooms. The rents varied from £2 to £4 per annum. Warwickshire farms were small. Farmers worked hard to produce poultry for the markets of the rapidly growing towns in the County. Although Warwickshire cheeses were once renowned, dairying gave way to breeding and rearing stock. Mixed breeds of cattle grazed in the fields because the farmers purchased the breed they considered most profitable for the current purpose. Large white pigs were bred, killed, cured and consumed in great numbers: it was customary for the artisans of Birmingham to keep pigs in their back yards. The polled Warwickshire sheep were crossed with Leicestershire rams and the heavy black horses were used for both cart and coach.

A greater part of the land was freehold with fairly rich soil, but life for the poor was equally grim in the town and the country (where in 1870 the average wage of a farm labourer was 12 shillings a week). A farm hand toiled all his life and starved in a hovel and when he could no longer work, a swift cheap burial in the church-yard was his reward. In time the struggles of Joseph Arch of Barford on behalf of the labourers successfully disturbed the peace of the County, and other counties throughout the kingdom. Joseph Arch commenced his fight in February 1872 with 5 shillings and he won it in April 1873 with a balance of £800 in Lloyds bank:

The men of Warwickshire, in the year of grace, eighteen hundred and seventy-two meant to stand up like soldiers and fight or die for the Agricultural Labourers Union.

Of course the farmers hit back at the Union men. At Radford and Wellesbourne the labourers were turned out of their cottages, and in Harbury and Snitterfield they were dismissed!

The principal canals which were first constructed in the eighteenth century brought to Birmingham and to other towns vital raw materials which included agricultural produce and took away the finished products to the sea-ports. The construction and progress of the railways encouraged fruit and vegetable growing in the Avon valley, but it was not long before the railway lines served the whole county. The wealthy tradesmen of Coventry and Birmingham quickly discovered that railway travel enabled them to move their businesses a little further along the line, just out of town. The new service also encouraged them to buy or rent a second home in the country.

Life for women in the household of a successful business man must have been comfortable but dull (even if a copy of Mrs Beeton's Cookery book could be purchased for 2 shillings). Entertainments included listening to religious sermons, visiting the sick and attending exhibitions! The ladies also enjoyed musical entertainment, deciphering gravestones in the local churchyard and reading such periodicals as *The Quiver*, in the evening by the fireside. Dining room suites in best leather could then be bought for £2-12-6d, and men could buy a made-to-measure suit in tweed or serge for 35/6d.

Gorse and heather colour the small stretches of heathland in the north of the County and they help in some measure to soften the stark colliery workings of the north-eastern area. Unhappily, by the end of the Edwardian era, the development of the colliery villages and the phenomenal growth of the cities of Birmingham and Coventry accounted for a decline of population in the rural parishes. Meanwhile many employers decided to take full advantage of the new railway system by building new factories adjacent to the railway lines. Before long new red-brick villas were built alongside, to house the employees. The town tramway systems extended their services to reach the new settlements and the third estate, the suburbs, was born.

Without the help of old photographs our knowledge of the Victorian and Edwardian periods would be sadly incomplete. It is particularly fitting therefore to pay tribute here to an enlightened Victorian gentleman, who had the initiative and skill to make a visual record of his age and to encourage others to follow his example. It was at a meeting of the Sutton Coldfield Vesey Club, in the year 1889, that William Jerome Harrison, a notable geologist, the science demonstrator to the Birmingham School Board and an amateur photographer, outlined his idea for making a photographic survey of Warwickshire. On 11 December Mr Harrison was invited by Sir Benjamin Stone to read to the Birmingham Photographic Society a paper entitled, 'Notes upon a proposed Photographic Survey of Warwickshire'. In his speech Mr Harrison stressed the importance of photographing ordinary people:

We must accumulate portraits, then, of all our local worthies. And to them we must add street scenes secured with the hand-camera from all our towns . . . from the country labourer in his smock-frock (a garment now rapidly disappearing) to the skilled artisan of the city, seated before his lathe. Nothing that illustrates contemporary life must be omitted – the policeman, the soldier, and the volunteer, must adorn our albums, and we must go slumming to depict the shady side of life.

The idea was seconded, resolved unanimously, and the Warwickshire Photographic Survey was born. The first meeting took place on 8 May 1890 and as a result of the remarkable team effort of the members, more than 10,000 photographs are now contained in the Local Studies Department of the Birmingham Central Libraries,

where they fulfill the purpose expressed – perhaps a little un-
expectedly – by the Countess of Warwick:

> . . . I am all in favour of fostering the local spirit. Make a man
> proud of and interested in, his birthplace or locality – make him feel
> he has a part in it – and you have started him on the road to good
> citizenship . . .

Frances Evelyn Warwick

5
Old men of Bidford, 1899

6 *right*
Mr J Mallard, Leamington's postman
from 1840 to 1879. It was his custom
when delivering letters to outlying
streets to summon the residents by the
lusty ringing of a bell

7
The stocks, Sutton Coldfield, drawn around the town on this occasion for the benefit of the photographer, Sir Benjamin Stone. The stocks still survive in a shelter opposite the Council House. 1895

8
Four generations of Healeys at New Hall, Sutton Coldfield, May 1895. At this time, New Hall was a boys' boarding school, and Thomas Everard Healey and his son, T. E. Healey, jnr. (standing) were its joint proprietors. New Hall, now again a private residence, is a moated manor house which claims to be the oldest home in England (reputedly dating from 1200)

9

Frances, Countess of Warwick, with her second son, the Hon. Maynard Greville. Lady Warwick, wife to Francis Greville, the fifth Earl of Warwick, was a famous Edwardian hostess and close friend of Edward VII. Well-known as a politician and philanthropist, she stood as Labour candidate for Warwick in 1923, polling 4,000 votes against the 16,000 of the Conservative, Anthony Eden (now Lord Avon). The author of several books, including a history of Warwick Castle and an edition of the autobiography of Joseph Arch, Lady Warwick founded, among other institutions, a girls' agricultural training college, a technical school, and a home for crippled children. Her conversion to socialism led to her renunciation of hunting and the wearing of furs and feathers; she became a vegetarian and sold her jewels to help finance Labour Party candidates. c.1900

10

Mr Edward Ansell and his family at home in the grounds of Moor Hall, Sutton Coldfield, 1907. Edward Ansell (1849–1929) was best known in the Birmingham area as managing director of the brewery at Aston Manor developed by his father Joseph from a small maltsters business into a major Midland firm, but he was also prominent in local government and philanthropic work, being for many years closely associated with the welfare of the old Borough of Aston

11
Warwickshire church cleaner, June
1897

12
The village of Ashow, where our reader sits, had a population of 133 people at this time. 1903

13
Jimmy Crump, soft-water seller, in High Street, Solihull. He offered his soft water (from a stream in Streetsbrook Road) at a halfpenny a bucket. The normal water supply at this time was from wells. 1870

14
Villagers at Meriden, the reputed centre of England. 1900

15
Old men at 'Drunken' Bidford, 1899,
possibly sampling a local home brew.
According to tradition, Shakespeare
patronised the Falcon Inn (now a private
house), where he lost a drinking contest
against the Bidford 'Sippers', the 'Top-
ers' being absent

16 *right*
An old man of Beaudesert, c.1890

17 *far right*
George Eliot (née Marian Evans, 1819–
90) was born at South Farm, Arbury,
near Nuneaton, being the daughter of
Robert Evans, the estate agent of
Francis Newdigate of Arbury Hall.
Educated at Attleborough, Nuneaton,
and Coventry, she set several of her
stories in Warwickshire, particularly
The Mill on the Floss (1860) and *Scenes
of Clerical Life* (1858)

18
Ice-cream seller in Smithfield Market,
Birmingham. 1901

20 *far left*
James Holliday, parish clerk and last of the Solihull beadles. Having served from 1861, he died on his way to church one Sunday evening in 1902, and was buried in his uniform. Though the post was latterly traditional rather than functional, his official duties were 'the maintenance of order and the chastisement of offenders'

21 *left*
Mr Elliston, Chief Librarian of Leamington (1863–4). The public library, among the country's earliest, was established in March 1857

19
Sewing at a cottage door, Little Virginia, Kenilworth, 1893

22
The River Anker in flood by the old
mill at Polesworth, December 1896

23 *left*
Delivery day for Alfred Byrne at the
Malt Shovel Hotel in Solihull High
Street, by the Henry Mitchell Brewery,
Cape Hill, Smethwick. The Royal Oak
Hotel and the Mason's Arms Inn can be
seen on the left of the photograph. c.
1890

24 *below left*
At the junction of High Street and
Coleshill Street, Sutton Coldfield, 1887,
when Mrs E. Archer kept the Royal Oak
and James Pittam kept the Old Sun. All
the old property below the church was
demolished in 1937 to make way for the
Vesey Memorial Gardens (opened in
1939), which commemorate the town's
great benefactor, John Vesey, Bishop of
Exeter (1452–1555), who presented
Sutton Park to the town and founded
the grammar school which still bears
his name

25
A chance meeting in Sandy Lane, Little
Bromwich, now called Ward End. 1891

26
In Aston, Birmingham, c. 1900

27
In Old Square, Birmingham, c. 1900, looking towards Upper Priory. Newbury's Store stands on the present site of Lewis's

28
Alcester High Street from the Church, 1865, when William Russen, home brewer, kept the Turk's Head

29
Town Hall and Esplanade, Leamington, c. 1900. Leamington owed its phenomenal growth and special architectural character to the quality of its curative thermal waters. These were first mentioned by Camden in 1586, the first bath being established in 1786. The population was 315 in 1800: by 1881 it was 23,000. The title 'Royal Leamington Spa' was authorised by Queen Victoria in 1838, and the Royal Baths and Pump Room were renovated in 1868. The Town Hall, designed by J. Cundall and completed in 1884, is tangible evidence of the civic pride of a firmly established town

31 *opposite left*
Butcher Row, Coventry, c. 1890, one of the numerous half-timbered Tudor streets which formed until quite recently a prominent feature of the city. While many perished in the blitz of the Second World War, some streets (including Butcher Row) had already disappeared in the central area redevelopment of the early 1930s

32 *opposite right*
At the Manor Farm, Preston Bagot, 30 May 1890. Formerly the property of the Earls of Warwick, then of Ingram Bagot, the village still retains its late sixteenth-century manor house which at the time of this photograph was occupied by Thomas Moore, farmer

30 *left*
A sunny day outside Warwick Castle, c. 1900

33
Artist at work. Welford-on-Avon, 1899

34 *left*
Calling at the Griffin Inn, Shustoke, 1897, when William Ancott, who was the farmer-publican, advertised good trout fishing from a nearby stream

35 *below left*
In the village of Arley, near Coventry, 1909

36
The Clock Tower, focal point of Rugby, c. 1910. In the background rises the spire of St Andrew's Church, which was added in 1895–6 to William Butterfield's extensions of 1877–85. The low embattled tower of the original fourteenth-century building may be seen to the right of the steeple

37
Beatrice and Frank Phelps, at 'Hilcote',
Leamington, October 1894

38
The life of Leamington in 1896 revealed by posters on the wall of Carr & Mason, stationers, at the junction of High Street and Bath Place

39
At the shop of Francis William Hawkesford, corn merchant, in Solihull High Street, c. 1910

40
Passing the shops in Aston, Birmingham, c. 1900

41
Looking towards the bottom of New Street, Birmingham, c. 1900

42
A fine display before the shop of Edwin Draper, fruiterer and greengrocer, Russell Terrace, Leamington, Christmas 1903

43
Backyard off Greenhill Street, Stratford, site of the present Picture House, c. 1900. These houses were demolished c. 1911–12

44
Linden Avenue, Leamington Spa. c. 1900

45
Nuneaton Market Place, c. 1910, when Mrs Helen Munton kept the Peacock Inn, and the Star Tea Company's delivery van stood before Ravenscroft & Sturgess, wine and spirit merchants

46
Stratford-upon-Avon High Street one midsummer morning in 1890. The Town Hall on the corner of Sheep Street and the Guild Hall can be seen in the far distance. The town lies on an ancient thoroughfare, 'the ford on the street'. At the beginning of the Victorian age, Stratford had a good corn market. The canals brought considerable quantities of grain and flour to Birmingham. Coal came by return carriage to Stratford. The river had been cleared, wharves laid out and warehouses built to enable communication with Gloucester, Bristol and Southern Ireland

47
Roasting a bullock at Stratford Mop Fair, 12 October 1895

48
Lt Col Joseph Henry Wilkinson, centre,
Mrs Wilkinson, and Joseph Bragg, at
the Wilkinsons' home, Ashfurlong Hall,
Sutton Coldfield, 11 September 1907.
Colonel Wilkinson (1845–1931) established the Cottage Hospital at Sutton,
and presented Barr Beacon to the public,
to be preserved permanently as an open
space

49
The Royal House Party at Coton, 3 July
1909. King Edward VII visited Rugby
to open the Temple Speech Room (in
memory of a former headmaster) at
Rugby School, staying at nearby Coton
House while visiting other places in the
county, including Birmingham, where
he opened the new University buildings
at Edgbaston in the same week. Edward
VII was the first monarch ever to visit
Rugby

50
Mr King, his sister, and their young
visitors at Peddimore Hall, Sutton
Coldfield, 1892

51
Augusta Jaques and Ada in their trap at
'The Dorridge', Knowle, 1891

52
Is it possible to smell home-baked bread, cakes and potatoes, yeast dumplings and rabbit stew in Thomas Fletcher's kitchen at Ramhall Farm, Berkswell? Colley free cooking pots in line can be seen on the shelf. 1892

53
At the village pump, wearing a human
yoke. 1900

54
Great activity at Middle Tysoe on an
April morning in 1895. This photograph
reveals the great variety of building
materials used and a degree of make-do
and mend. The chief crops grown at
this time were wheat and beans, but
most of the land was used for grazing.
A certain William Heritage was both
the village butcher and baker at this
time

55
Chopping wood at Water Orton, 1893

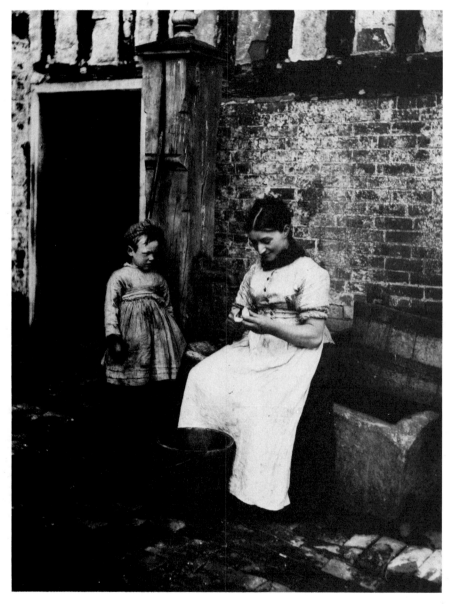

56
Peeling potatoes at Poplar Farm, Knowle.
Mrs Polly Wood and daughter, 6 April
1890

57
Village gossips at Barston, near Solihull,
4 April 1890

STRATFORD

58 *overleaf*

The Shakespeare Memorial Theatre, Stratford, from across the Avon, 1899. The move to build a permanent theatre followed on the 1864 tercentenary of Shakespeare's birth, and the successful completion of the theatre in 1879 was due largely to the enthusiasm and generosity of the Flower family (local brewers). Designed by Dodgshun and Unsworth in a High Victorian Gothic style, it opened on 23 April (the poet's birthday) with a performance of *Much Ado about Nothing*. Its architectural style, never widely popular, was likened by Marie Corelli to 'a brewer's vat', and on its destruction by fire in 1925 G. B. Shaw sent a telegram of congratulation. The present theatre was completed in 1932 and continues to present a series of Shakespeare's plays each season

59

Shakespeare's Birthplace before restoration, as it was in 1846. The Birthplace had passed out of the poet's family in 1806; but the Garrick Jubilee of 1769 had greatly encouraged tourism in Stratford, and the two widows, Mrs Hornby and Mrs Court, who successively controlled the property, did much to bring the Shakespeare industry into disrepute with their extravagant anecdotes and bogus relics. By the time both widows had died, the house, now divided into an inn (the Swan and Maidenhead) and a butcher's shop, was in a serious state of disrepair, and only its purchase for the nation by the Birthplace Trust saved it from eventual collapse. In an early and far-sighted instance of conservation work, the Trust had restored the house by 1858

60

A crowd coming to the theatre, c. 1900

61

The Quiney House, c. 1890, at this time the shop of Edward Fox, bookseller, stationer and printer and clearly a significant contributor to the rapidly growing tourist industry. Originally known as The Cage (being on the site of a former gaol), it was once the home of Thomas Quiney, a wine merchant, who married Shakespeare's younger daughter Judith in 1616. The house has undergone several changes of function, being restored in 1923 and subsequently becoming a café and (its present function) the Stratford Tourist Information Centre

62

Procession of local citizens and visitors to lay wreaths on Shakespeare's tomb (in Holy Trinity Church), 23 April 1900. This birthday tribute is now an annual event. The first organised Shakespeare celebrations were held on the occasion of the Garrick Jubilee in 1769, and stemmed from the erection of Stratford Town Hall and the granting of the freedom of the borough to the Shakespearean actor David Garrick. In its modern form, however, the Shakespeare Festival dates from the time Frank Benson took over the theatre in 1886

63

'Pied Piper' play at the Stratford Shakespeare Festival, 30 July 1910. Of the old Memorial Theatre in the background only the gabled art gallery to the left of the picture now survives

64
Performers from *A Midsummer Night's Dream* outside the Shakespeare Memorial Theatre, June 1906

66
The Tom Fool of the Bidford Morris Dancers at the celebrations for Shakespeare's Birthday, April 1904

65
Mr and Mrs F. R. Benson and Mr R. Halford Foster at Stratford Shakespeare Festival, April 1906. Frank Benson (1858–1939), having played under Irving at the Lyceum, was appointed director of the Shakespeare Festival in 1886, and for the next thirty years firmly established this in its recognisably modern form. He extended the festival from Shakespeare's birthday well into the summer, and made it his policy to produce as many of the plays as possible, even an uncut *Hamlet*. His actors were encouraged to participate in sport ('Send a good fast bowler to play Laertes.') Benson enjoyed tremendous popularity in Stratford, his carriage being pulled through the streets each time he arrived at the station. He was the first manager to choose for provincial tours those Shakespeare plays currently featuring in local school curricula. For his services to the theatre, he was knighted by George V at Drury Lane in 1916

67
Marie Corelli (née Mary Mackay, 1855–1924), at the window of her home, Mason Croft (now the Shakespeare Institute of the University of Birmingham), where she lived from 1901 to 1924. One of the most popular novelists of her day, she was noted for her sensational treatment of religious themes (e.g. in *Barabbas* and *The Sorrows of Satan*). While at Stratford, she was involved in fierce controversy with many local and national figures, and became notable in the town for her eccentricities, sailing in a gondola (complete with Venetian gondolier) upon the Avon. Her fervent admiration for Shakespeare was matched only by her enthusiasm for her own works, which she kept in a special bookcase and offered as bedside reading to her guests. Her opposition to various redevelopment projects in the town resulted, however, in some valuable conservation and restoration work

69
Hanging out washing behind a house in
Sheep Street, 1899

68
Stratford Parish Church, seen from the
garden of Mrs Charles Flower (seated).
The Flower family were Stratford's
most prominent citizens throughout the
Victorian and Edwardian period. The
foundation, by Edward Fordham Flower
in 1831, of the brewery in Birmingham
Road, Stratford, began a long tradition
of industrial, cultural and philanthropic
service to the town. Edward Fordham
Flower was particularly interested in
the welfare of horses, seeking to prevent
the cruel application of bearing reins
and gag-bits; but the best-known
achievement of the family is un-
doubtedly the gift to the town of the
Shakespeare Memorial Theatre, the
original building being opened in 1879
at the personal expense of Charles
Edward Flower on land provided by
him. Also in the picture (centre) is Sir
Benjamin Stone (1838–1914), the Birmingham industrialist and politician, best
known today as a pioneer of 'record
photography'. 1896

70
Restoring the almshouses at Stratford in 1902. This work, though undertaken by the Corporation, was largely financed by Mrs Sarah Flower

71
Richard Wyatt, an inmate of the almshouses and formerly Mayor of the town
(1899)

72
Inmate of Stratford Almshouses, 1899

73
Stratford-on-Avon Market, then held in
Bridge Street, c. 1890. On the left is the
Red Horse Hotel, where Washington
Irving wrote his *Sketchbook* (1820). A
market has been held in Stratford since
1196

74
Roasting a pig in Henley Street at the
Mop Fair of October 1895. Shakespeare's
Birthplace, in the restored form familiar
today, rises in the background

75
Laying the foundation stone of the
Public Library in Henley Street, 1902.
Part of the Tudor house already on the
site was incorporated in the new
building

76
Village children at Studley (1897), when the chief manufactures were needles, bodkins, and fishing tackle

77
Children of the village of Haselor at play. Good quantities of wheat, barley and beans grow in the rich marl soil. Nearby Mrs Ann Knight ran her cider mill. The thatchers' work was measured in 10 ft by 10 ft squares. The floors of the old timbered houses usually consisted of clay and cow-dung (puddled), while between the timbers willow and hazel branches were woven basket-like and then were covered with a layer of clay and cow-dung. August, 1892

78 *opposite*
Dance of the 'fairies' taking part in *A Midsummer Night's Dream* at Stratford Shakespeare Festival, 12 June 1906, beside the River Avon

79 *opposite left*
Two little maids playing a game of 'let's pretend' in Paradise Row, Halford. Fanny Jacques, their schoolmistress, has told them all about growing up in an old village, which takes its name from an ancient ford close to the Roman way. Their parents would remember seeing the gentry bowling on the famous green, but if you entered the Bell Inn, the landlord, James Pannett, would discuss the Stour and Foss Football Club with pride. 1896

80 *opposite right*
Children at work beneath caged linnets. Annie Mold, the schoolmistress of Haselor, reported that out of 60 children in the village, only an average of 25 attended school! 1892

81
Village children and their teacher at
Astley, 1899

82
A class in Mason's Orphanage, Erdington, Birmingham, 1908

83
Village children at Water Orton in 1893. The boys, wearing their elder sisters' outgrown dresses, reflect a practice quite common among the poorer people at this time, particularly in rural areas

84
Village children at Hurley, May 1895

85
Rugby School, from the Close, c. 1906. Founded in 1567 by Lawrence Sheriff, a merchant grocer and servant to Queen Elizabeth, and originally intended for local children, the school stood in the first instance opposite the parish church, moving to its present site in 1740–50. The present buildings are predominantly nineteenth century, having been planned by Henry Hakewill and William Butterfield. The school's great days were those of Dr Thomas Arnold (headmaster 1828–42) and Dr Frederick Temple (1857–69). Arnold's programme of 'firstly religious principles, secondly gentlemanly conduct, thirdly intellectual ability' had a profound effect upon the subsequent development of public schools. Arnold's Rugby is the subject of an Old Boy's novel, *Tom Brown's Schooldays* (1857, by Thomas Hughes), and the school chapel is the subject of a poem by the headmaster's son, Matthew Arnold (1822–88)

86
The staff of Rugby School, c. 1910,
when Dr H. A. James (centre, front
row) was headmaster

87
An agricultural worker between en-
gagements; probably he is waiting for
a lift from a friendly wagoner at the
crossroads. 20 June 1891

88
Reaping at Kineton, where the worker
is seen using the stick and crook
method, not far away from the battle-
field of Edgehill. c. 1890

89
Farm labourer at Wolvey, near Nuneaton, 1896

90
Milking at Kineton. The land produced good wheat and beans but it was not considered good grazing land. The thin animal photographed here seems to prove the point. c. 1889

91
Sheep-shearing, 1895

92
The skill of the wheelwright was vital to a village community and Richard Holmes Thompson performed the task in Balsall Street in 1890. A journeyman could earn as much as a guinea or thirty shillings a week. 1890

93
A good crop at 'Papist' Wixford, a village on the Arrow. It is reasonable to assume that one horse in the team was called 'Blossom' and the cry 'Haw dam yer' would be heard as they struggled home looking forward to a drink with Mrs Fanny Hopkins at her pub, the Three Horse Shoes. 1889

94

The wagon team pauses in the village of Newton Regis, near Tamworth, on a fine June day. The shafts of each wagon were skilfully tapered for balance and such a vehicle cost between £50 and £60. 1891

95

Mr Thomas Morris, the farmer, using his horse rake at Fen End, 1902

96

Mr Mercer, the Squire of Water Orton, breaking in his horse 'Raven', June 1892

97

All the family reaping the wheat at Tredington on 5 August 1901. It was a slow process. The corn was grasped just below the heads in the left hand and cut as low as possible with a sickle. Each handful was carefully laid together by the reaper and bound into sheaves by the women; about six 'shucks' were stood up together to dry before being loaded on the wain. As the last load left the fields the women were allowed to glean the remains, which in War-wickshire was called 'leasing'

98
Labourers wearing whipcords indicating they seek employment as carters at Stratford Mop, 1899. Formerly, Stratford had boasted eleven fairs; but by the turn of the century there were only two, the second of which – the 'Mop' – was said to be the largest statute fair in England. At this time, the Mop Fair (which is still held) was regarded by agricultural workers as the chief holiday of the year. It was one of the few remaining hiring fairs (a custom of Roman origin), and the prevalence of whipcord (the trademark of the carter) indicated that carters were much in demand. Such men offered themselves for inspection by local employers, and the farmers were accustomed to feel the labourers' muscles in search of 'a likely lad'

99
Workmen setting retorts at the Birmingham Gas Works, 1896. The history of gas lighting in Birmingham began with the experiments made by William Murdoch in 1798. He gave the first public display at Soho in 1802. Birmingham's first gas works were erected by John Gosling in 1817. Gosling's business was acquired by the Birmingham Gas Light Company in 1825. Another business was established called the Birmingham and Staffordshire Gas Light Company. Due to the efforts of Joseph Chamberlain all gas interests were acquired by the Corporation of Birmingham in 1875

100
Memorial card to P. C. Hine, of the
Warwickshire Police, 1886

101
Supt Lee, Stratford-on-Avon Division,
with his groom, P.C. Bazeley, 1912

102
The old Post Office, Solihull High
Street, c. 1900

103
Cutting the wood at the wheelwright's shop, Curdworth, 1895. Mr Joseph Moore was the wheelwright at this time. By tradition sawyers were considered to be temperamental.

104
Mr Blackwell's Forge, Henley-in-Arden, c. 1900

105
The Vittoria Street School for Jewellers and Silversmiths in Birmingham was specially intended for those engaged in the jewellery and kindred trades – brassworkers, chain-makers, chasers, clerks, damasceners, designers, die-sinkers, enamellers, engravers, gold-smiths, jewellers, jewellers' case-makers, lapidaries, makers of electro-plate, mounters, repoussé workers, setters, silversmiths, stampers, tool-makers, travellers, warehousemen and any others concerned with the metal trades – and other students were ad-mitted if space allowed. The head-master was Mr R. Catterson-Smith. The photograph shows the afternoon session at work in the metal shop. 1902

106
J. Green's 'photographic cart' near Hampton-in-Arden, c. 1880. Such port-able studios were common at this time

107
Boating on the moat at Peddimore Hall, Sutton Coldfield, 1907. The Hall was at one time the seat of the Ardens, Shakespeare's maternal ancestors

108
Dorridge Bowling Club, June 1891

109
Meet of the North Warwickshire Fox-
hounds outside Wootton Wawen Hall.
Fifty couples of hounds were kept in
Roundshill Lane, Kenilworth. Hunting
days were Tuesdays, Wednesdays, Fri-
days and sometimes Saturdays. At this
period, Warwickshire ranked third as a
hunting district among the counties of
England, and Leamington was considered to be the most important centre.
1905

110 *below*
Henley-in-Arden Quoits Club, 1905

111 *opposite top*
Playing hockey in 1898: Erdington v. Leicester

112 *opposite middle*
Skating on Windley Pool, Sutton Park, 1892. Sutton Park, formerly Crown Land and originally the property of the Earls of Warwick, was presented to the citizens of Sutton Coldfield by Bishop Vesey in 1528. During the nineteenth century, the natural attractions of the Park, aided by the coming of the railway, made Sutton into a popular tourist centre for the West Midlands, numerous hotels, guest-houses and tea-rooms springing up. In 1870, a cheap rail excursion was offered from Birmingham to Sutton Coldfield 'every day during the Frost. Fare there and back including admission to the Royal Promenade and Windley Pool, 9d. Covered carriages'

113 *opposite bottom*
Archery used to be an integral part of the forest life of England. Centuries ago the male population of each village assembled at the 'Butts' to practise. At the Bull's Head, Meriden, on 15 November 1785, the ancient skills were revived. The archers were captained by the Earl of Aylesford, who became Perpetual Warden. The style of dress was decided on: green coat, white waistcoat and breeches with the Arden button. In the photograph, the Scottish Archers of Her Majesty's Bodyguard are seen meeting with the Woodmen of Arden at Meriden, 1897

114
Rugby School v. Cheltenham, 9 December 1907. In the Doctor's Wall, at the School, a plaque commemorates William Webb Ellis, 'who with a fine disregard for the rules of football as played in his time first took the ball in his arms and ran with it, thus originating the distinctive feature of the Rugby game, AD 1823'

115
Skittles at the Queen and Castle Inn, Kenilworth, 1901

116
Croquet on the lawn at Driffold House, Sutton Coldfield, c. 1900

117
Morris dancers in the garden of Mrs Charles Flower, Stratford-on-Avon, 1904. Such dances were regular features at the Mop Fair, and took the form of the 'hay', a dance whose name is believed to have been derived from the French *haie* (hedge). The dancers stood in two rows recalling parallel hedges. The performers also danced in a circle, moving from the circle, winding round, handing in passing until they returned to their original places

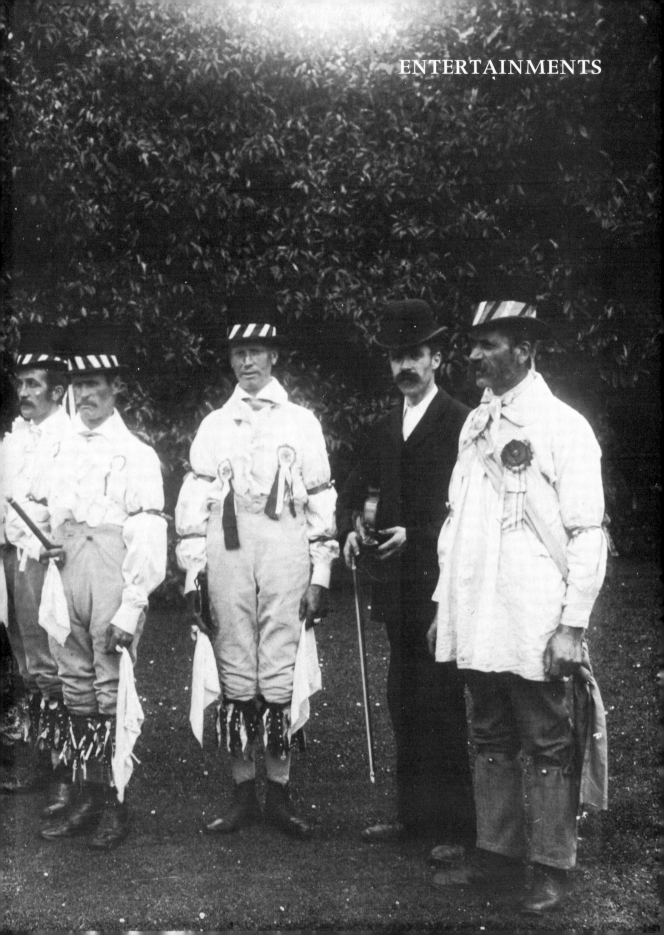

118

Ox-roast at Stratford Mop Fair, in 1899. The 'Mop' is believed to derive its name from the fact that it was at one time the second hiring fair of the year, at which the 'refuse' from the first fair was mopped or swept up. At the Mop's street barbecues, as many as a dozen improvised cooking ranges would be set up, with laid tables before them, and as many as half a dozen oxen and a dozen pigs would be cut up and served at each fair. From the brick fireplaces the meat was sold in portions to the passers-by, the average annual takings being at this time around £80

119

Mrs T. Whaley, at Birmingham Dog Show (1905), with her prizewinning griffon dog and bitch

120
Pig-roast at Bidford Mop, 1899

121
Dancing bears outside Solihull Church, c. 1900

122
Schoolchildren at a rehearsal for Warwick Pageant, 1906

123
The Vesey Club at Maxstoke Castle, near Coleshill, at this time (1906) the residence of Harold Lincoln Tangye, JP. This fourteenth-century moated mansion is still inhabited

124
Awaiting the May Queen at Dunchurch
Market Cross, c. 1900

125
Performance at a garden party at
Middleton Hall, 1904. This ancient
mansion, lying between Tamworth and
Coleshill, was tenanted at this time by
Egbert de Hamel, Lord Middleton being
lord of the manor and principal land-
owner

126
Calling at the George Hotel, Solihull,
c. 1910, when the licensee was Eliza
Hillman. This sixteenth-century inn is
still noted for its fine bowling green

127
Warwick-Leamington horse tram, c. 1900. The service ran from 1880 to 1905

128
A scene on the Birmingham canal near Lapworth. The Act for this canal was passed in March 1793. It was opened, together with the Warwick and Napton canal, on 19 December 1799. (c. 1900)

129
The canal burst at Great Charles Street, Birmingham, 1903

130
Building the Great Central Railway (now itself defunct) over the canal, between Brownsover Mill and Vicarage Hill, Clifton. The building of this line, the last main railway route to be completed, gave Rugby access to the north-east and south-west. Work began in 1895, and the first train passed through Rugby in 1898

131
A trimming gang at Brownsover, near Rugby, c. 1895. These navvies made the ground level before the permanent way was laid

132
Building the railway station at Henley-in-Arden, 1894. Plans for a Henley Railway dated from 1861; but it was not until 1894 that the Birmingham and Henley-in-Arden Railway completed their extension from the Birmingham-Oxford line. Henley Station was subsequently absorbed into the North Warwickshire line (Birmingham-Stratford), which opened in 1908, and the link with the Oxford line was severed in 1915

133
Queen Victoria's train passing through
Olton Station, after Her Majesty had
laid the foundation stone of the Victoria
Law Courts, Birmingham. 23 March
1887

134 *overleaf*
A giant signalling installation of the
LNWR at Rugby. Erected in 1896, this
44-arm signal gantry was the largest in
the British Isles. It was removed when
electric colour light signalling was
installed in October, 1939. The early
construction of the GCR steel girder
bridge (designed to cross the LNWR
line) can be seen in the photograph

135
Local volunteers at Rugby Midland Station, attending the departure of King Edward VII (July, 1909). This station (still substantially the same) was opened by the LNWR in 1886. It was the third station to be built in Rugby, and is now the only one remaining, being the original of Dickens' 'Mugby Junction'

136
Mr F. H. Pepper and children calling at the Grange, Erdington, 1903

137
A call at The Grange, Erdington, home
of Sir Benjamin Stone, Christmas 1902.
Left to right: Hartley Yates, Norman
Stone, Fred Perks Yates, Beatrice Yates,
Mrs Oscar Stone, Barron Stone

138
Political garden party at The Grange,
Erdington, Birmingham, home of Sir
Benjamin Stone, 1901. Stone, a tireless
Conservative Party worker, was
Knighted for his political services

139
The Royal Reception Party on the platform of Rugby Midland Station, awaiting the arrival of King Edward VII, 3 July 1909

140
A Jubilee dinner for old people held in a tent adjoining the Town Hall, Sutton Coldfield, 24 June 1887

141
Empire Day at Alveston, near Stratford (1905)

142
Lady Godiva rides along Warwick Row, Coventry on 7 August 1907. The part was enacted by a music hall artist called 'La Milo'. Her horse was clad in blue and gold and no less than thirty special trains ran to Coventry for the occasion

143
The reception in the garden of the Grange, Erdington, after the wedding of Dora Stone and Dr MacKenzie, 19 July 1899

144
A celebrity comes to Stratford: Mark
Twain arrives in his motor car, c. 1900

145
Sailing down Attleborough Road, Nuneaton (1900). Nuneaton, a low-lying town, has been subject to frequent flooding

146
The funeral of Alderman S. T. Wackrill, of Leamington, 16 May 1907

147
The Duke and Duchess of York passing through Hedge Hill Common, Birmingham, 1895

148
Recruiting posters in Birmingham 1914

149
The Golden Jubilee procession moving towards Sutton Park, passing along the High Street and about to enter Mill Street (1887). To the left of the picture may be seen the Three Tuns Hotel, reputedly a halting place for Shakespeare's Falstaff ('Fill me a bottle of sack : our soldiers shall march through; we'll to Sutton Cofil tonight')

150
Mr and Mrs Joseph Chamberlain at Chamberlain's seventieth birthday celebrations in Ward End Park, Birmingham (1906). Joseph Chamberlain (1836–1914), beginning as a prosperous Birmingham screw manufacturer, retired at the age of thirty-eight to devote himself full-time to politics. A radical and energetic councillor, he was Mayor of Birmingham from 1873 to 1876, and – apart from his important slum clearance programme culminating in the construction of Corporation Street – was responsible for numerous reforms, including the development of free libraries and galleries, state education, and the establishment in Birmingham of a Corporation gasworks, waterworks, and sewage farm. Elected Liberal MP for Birmingham in 1876, he was responsible for much important legislation at national level, and for a thorough reorganisation of the Liberal Party machine. Leaving the Liberals in 1886 over the Home Rule question, he subsequently became a Conservative MP, latterly distinguishing himself in the rôle of Colonial Secretary

151
The christening of Frederick Knight
Wynn at Whateley Hall, Castle Brom-
wich, 1 August 1906

152

Drinking the health of the Duke of Buccleuch (in glasses of rum and milk) at the Dun Cow, Ryton-on-Dunsmore, after the Wroth money Ceremony, 11 November 1899. The Wroth Money is collected before sunrise on the nearby Knightlow Hill each St Martin's Day by an agent of the Duke of Buccleuch as 'Lord of the Hundreds of Knightlow'. The amount collected from the twenty-eight parishes affected was only ten, shillings at this time. The Duke's agent, in collecting the tribute, stands facing east, and begins by reading the 'Charter of Assembly', after which each parish representative, as the name of his parish is called, casts the required sum into the hollow base of an ancient wayside cross. Said to date from Saxon times, the Wroth Money Ceremony is believed to have originated partly as an acknowledgment of the claim of the lord of the manor to the waste lands within the Hundred, and partly as a tax for the rights of way of cattle from one village to another. Those who have paid the tribute are afterwards invited by the agent to a substantial breakfast at the Duke's expense.

153
The end of an era. Horses of the Royal
Artillery tethered in Greatheed Road,
Leamington, during mobilisation of the
29th Division before sailing for Gallipoli
(Spring, 1915)